GW00720398

...A unique and inventive collection
Sounds

...The importance of the anthology is that it represents twentieth century multi-ethnic poetries – radically engaged with, and responsive to what's happening now. More please! *City Limits*

Poetry as performance is an area that has tended to be gravely neglected in recent years. Apples and Snakes ... seem to have gone a long way towards rectifying that situation *The Stage*

This book says it all *Time Out*

Everything about this book is exciting *The Voice*

First published in 1984 by **Pluto Press Limited,**
The Works, 105a, Torriano Avenue, London NW5 2RX
and **Pluto Press Australia Limited,**
PO Box 199, Leichhardt, New South Wales 2040, Australia

Second impression 1984

Illustrations by **Steve Lobb**

Text and cover designed by **Neville Brody**
Typeset by **Promenade Graphics Ltd., Cheltenham, Gloucestershire**
Printed in Britain by **Photobooks (Bristol) Limited**
Bound by **W.H. Ware & Sons Limited, Clevedon, Avon**

British Library Cataloguing in Publication Data
Apples and snakes.
  1. English poetry—20th century
  821'.914'08   PR1225

ISBN 0-86104-753-2

APPLES AND SNAKES

Raw and Biting Cabaret Poetry

PLUTO PRESS

CONTENTS

Apples and Snakes, what exactly are apples and snakes? No doubt you are asking yourselves. Well, snakes are brown leather objects which some people (usually bedwetters and myopic freight journalists) wear on their feet. Sometimes they have laces. However, apples are a primitive type of portable fan heater. This information enables you to understand the Book of Genesis properly, it also explains why London's best poetry cabaret is not called brown shoes and primitive fan heaters—it would be too long. Therefore the non-sexist management collective (Chris Cardale, Bernie Cunnane, Chris Flanagan, P.R. Murry and Mandy Williams) opted for the more conventional Apples and Snakes.

If you go to Apples and Snakes now you go to the Roebuck pub on Tottenham Court Road, London, but there's going to be a British tour and yes, Apples and Snakes will be coming to you soon. You will find yourself in a sweaty crowded smoky room where the audience listens to people speaking. It could be said the performers speak poetry and entertain people, but a lot of them would disagree with this description because they shout, scream, bellow, boom, rant, roar, rave and whisper, they also murmur, throb and pulsate. They reinforce their words with stage craft and charisma, with manic gesticulations and convulsed dance-like movements; or come across as deadpan as a cracked scaffold plank. The compères have tape loops of annoying drivel which they repeat night after night after night, some are inebriates, some are hairy and some of them get annoyed and tell the audience off for not immediately appreciating impeccably Marxist-Leninist sound-poetry.

In England poetry has been dominated by a small clique who all wear brown shoes and don't think a poem is a poem unless it contains words which no one else can understand. Apples and Snakes has for over a year put on shows for people who aren't interested in that kind of crap and has proved that words are contagious, in fact they are an epidemic. At Apples and Snakes' second night in the Roebuck, the landlord said to a member of the non-sexist collective that he'd cracked it. He wasn't talking about his kneecap, his was the only pub on Tottenham Court Road to have a full bar on Saturday nights. He thought they were running a dirty show when he saw how many people were in there, but they explained all they'd got was some geezer up on stage doing *Hickory Dickory Dock*.

From then on Apples and Snakes knew they were right, poetry is a living art form, it talks to people, it makes electric and chemical currents fire in their brain cells, it awakes obscure memories and tired taste buds, it rots the toenails of pompous fools, so there . . .

AFRICAN DAWN: The African Dawn come from Ghana, Senegal, Zimbabwe and Kenya. For the last few years they have entertained, educated and inspired audiences in Britain. Their work signifies a dawn of authentic cultural expression from minds and voices that have defied colonial suffocation. Their work can be found on an album *Besiege the Night*.

JOHN AGARD: His work takes its pulse from the oral tradition and as a performer he calls himself a poetsonian, a word he uses because he feels a kinship with the rhythms of the calypsonian. Since coming to England in 1977, he has had three children's books published and gives talks to schools for the Commonwealth Institute.

ALEV: Born in Instanbul. Half Turkish. Twenty years old. 5'4". Now lives in London and is a member of the Communist Party.

ANDY P: Born in Leeds and brought up a Catholic, joined the Communist Party eight years ago. Lives in North London with life-partner and cat, star striker for Hackney Red Star FC, likes the colour red, hot baths and Italy, dislikes most other things.

FERENC ASZMANN: Once v. stupid/twenty-five years old; S.E. London wordsmith; since sixteen onstages including rockvenues and other British mental institutions including Last butmost RealLife/Currently dialecticizing between paperdevil of H.M. Culture and shallow grey sea of new Socialist Realisms/confident that, on realvolutionary road, redhotrods with vizzions are worth x easy laughs in emptypistols.

ATTILA THE STOCKBROKER: Ranting poet and troubadour. Album on Cherry Red *Ranting at the Nation*. New album *Sawdust and Empire*. Book with Seething Wells published 1984. Ranting poetry magazine *Tirana Thrash* featuring many new up-and-coming poets available from 161 Spencers Croft, Harlow, Essex.

MICHAEL BELBIN: B. 1956. Playwright/screenwriter. Performed 'cut-out'/ surrealist poetry 1976. Present phase began 1982. Major influences— Auden, Brecht, haiku, Irish POWs, PolyStyrene.

CHRIS CARDALE: Unemployed, assistant muralist, mosaicist, irrigation worker, undertaker's assistant, milkman, exam-passer, recent joint leader of 'under the nose'—a workshop for the creative expression of children. Own book *U-I Poems*; doing performance poems for four years.

DONAL CARROLL: Born republic of Ireland; worked at various jobs in England including teaching and television servicing; has written books, articles, reviews and poetry for various magazines; believes poetry should occupy a fuller world and be more exciting (and political) than an evening out with the SDP.

ANNE CLARK: Twenty-three. First concert at Richard Strange's Cabaret Futura in London 1979. Toured all over England and Belgian tours in 1982 and 1983. Full length LP *Changing Places* released in 1983. Wrote script for

Isolation, a film for Channel 4 to be shown in 1984.

PAT CONDELL: Born Ireland 1949. Grew up in South London. After travelling in Europe, the Middle East and North America he spent five years as a labourer in western Canada. A founder member of the comedy group Mountbatten's Plimsoll, he now performs alone and regularly contributes a poem to the London magazine *Time Out*.

KEVIN COYNE: Poet/singer. Has released twenty LPs, currently working with Rough Trade in Germany. In the process of forming his own record company through Rough Trade.

BERNIE CUNNANE: Has been writing poetry for many years and takes as her subject matter situations and observed incidents in such diverse places as Tesco's, the drawing office and conversations overheard on buses. Her ambition is to be the first person to earn a salary merely for being alive.

PATRICK CUNNANE: Born in the 1950s of Irish parents. In recent years has worked with the performance groups Worthless Words and Tongue Circus. A first collection *Roads* in collaboration with Hertfordshire poet Patrick Holley was published by Badger Books. A new collection *Butterfly in the Shithouse* is expected in 1984.

CLAIRE DOWIE: Lives in Wandsworth, London, with her dog, who has a penchant for chewing electrical flex, Claire has a penchant for mending electrical flex so it's a very complementary relationship.

ALISON FELL: Born in Scotland. Has worked in women's centres, street theatre, the underground press, on *Spare Rib*, and as a writer in residence in schools. She has published poetry in several anthologies and also two novels—*The Grey Dancer* (Collins) and *Every Move You Make* (Virago).

ALAN GILBEY: Born 1958 and educated in the East End where he first wrote poetry. In 1977 he co-founded the theatre/comedy/poetry group Controlled Attack. He has a book *Singalongattax* which is available from Thap Bookshop, 178 Whitechapel Rd, London E1.

GINGER JOHN THE DOOMSDAY COMMANDO: Born Manchester, lives Bradford. Own book *Ranting of the Barricades* recently unleashed. Gigging since mid 1982 with ranting poets and supporting bands including Chelsea, Peter & the Test Tube Babies and the Newtown Neurotics.

JOHN HEGLEY: Born Islington 1/10/53. Most precious possession— spectacles. Most prestigious professional engagement—John Peel session with Popticians. Likes: sensitivity, sensuality, beer.

MARKUS JAHN: A poet, philosopher and writer of reality which manifests itself in the omnipotent mind of such man, Markus Jahn; to reveal within his works, through words and Imotions, the sufferation of mankind throughout the four corners of Iration, and to reflect such man experience of 'dwellin' eena Babylon eena dis time'.

DENISE KING: Some things surrounding D.K. at the time of writing: Beethoven's Piano Sonato Op.111 C Minor (playing); a photograph of a Volcano Rabbit (conservation); books—*Anne Boleyn, The Vampire, Brave New World*. Is this a portrait of the artist as a young woman?

FRAN LANDESMAN: Songwriter and cabaret artist who has appeared at Ronnie Scott's, Riverside Studios and other dives too numerous to plug. Published four volumes of verse and often pops up in anthologies for the edification of the young.

LITTLE DAVE: Writing poetry for three years, gigging for two and a half years round London. TV and radio appearances. Has worked with Wet Paint Theatre Co. for their production, *Love's a Revolution*

DINAH LIVINGSTONE: Lives in Camden Town (since 1966). Frequently says poems in public London and elsewhere. Collections include: *Ultrasound* (1975); *Prepositions and Conjunctions* (1977); *Love in Time* (1982); *Glad Rags* (1983). All available from Katabasis, 10 St Martin's Close, London NW1.

GLADYS MCGEE: Has written poetry for years. Has performed it with great success locally and nationally. She is a pensioner who has long been involved with the Basement Writers and has a book *Shoutin' and Bawlin'* which is available from Thap Bookshop.

RORY MCLEOD: Returned to London in 1981 after six years' migrant work abroad. Worked as a musical clown, fire-eater, labourer, mariachi—won the Texas Harmonica Championship. A singer songwriter, 'Criminals of Hunger' is a song written for the Guerrilla fighters in Guatemala, El Salvador, also inspired by the riots in Britain in 1981.

JENNIFER MITCHELL: Featured in the *City Lines* anthology of poems by London school students, her work has also appeared in *Spare Rib*.

PETE MURRY: Has been writing on and off and one or two other words for a bit now. Has been involved with Worthless Words and Tongue Circus, and now performs solo.

OWEN O'NEILL: I'm quite a good runner—it's good for you, keeps you healthy. I run a poetry venue, the 'Tongue Out Of Cheek' at the Star & Garter, Putney Bridge. Poetry runs in my family, so do legs.

STEF PIXNER: Born in London in 1945 and now lives in London with friends. She also writes songs and is working on a novel.

MARSHA PRESCOD: Is a young black woman who came to England as part of the great wave of settlers from the Caribbean in the late 1950s The underlying theme of her poems is usually political but she uses humour where she can because 'it can be honed into a deadly weapon and why should Reagan have all the fun?'

JAY RAMSAY: Is writing a long poem in a series of connected books, each of which explores a developing structure. Begun in 1980. Three so far completed. 1981: created various mixed evenings under the working title

Knife in the Light. Co-founded the Angels of Fire collective. Edits the *Third Eye* and reviews in *City Limits.*

MICHELE ROBERTS: Lives and works in London. Besides writing and teaching part-time she performs her poetry at a wide range of cabaret, pubs and other venues all around the country. Most recent book of poetry with Judith Kazantis and Michelene Wandor is *Touch Papers* (Allison & Busby). Most recent novel *The Visitation* (Women's Press).

JOHN ROWE: Born 1947 Barking, Essex. Books: *Yawn, Stewed Tea and Breadcrumbs, Shout, Arrested Development, Where there's Muck* and *John Relic versus the Ranters.* Toured with Stereo Graffiti mid 1970s. Has worked with many East Anglian reggae and punk bands and visits numerous schools in the Eastern region.

EMILE SERCOMBE: Trained as a painter, taught art for some years and exhibited pictures and soft sculptures; started writing poetry with Worthless Words in 1980 and went on to perform with Tongue Circus. Now working on 'Supermarket—futuresaga' and painting external murals.

SPARTACUS R: International musician from Grenada, West Indies. Co-founded Osibisa in 1969, creating a new category of music (Afro-Rock). In 1981 decided to go solo. First solo album *Africa I See. Third World War* his latest album.

MARK STEEL: First professional poetry performance was the now legendary 'Animal Alphabet' at a holiday camp under-sevens' talent contest but has since become a successful comedian, sometimes performing to as few as three people.

NICK TOCZEK: Writer and performer. Has eleven books out, latest being *Rock 'n' Roll Terrorism.* One single with the band Ulterior Motives. Cassette LP on Blurgh Tapes, *The Britanarchist Demo.* Freelance columnist in north of England and writes for national music weeklies. Runs rock and cabaret clubs in Leeds area. Born and lives in Bradford.

MICHELENE WANDOR: Poet, playwright, critic; poetry editor of *Time Out* 1971–82. Recent publications include *Upbeat* (poems and stories, including 'Some Male Poets', Journeyman), *Understudies* (theatre and sexual politics, Methuen) and *On Gender and Writing* (Pandora).

FREDERICK WILLIAMS: Jamaican—writer and publisher of poems and short stories. Has read extensively in various venues, also on radio and TV in Great Britain and the Caribbean.

BENJAMIN ZEPHANIAH: Born in Jamaica and came to this country aged seven. Learnt his craft while in the nick for street crime. Performs all over the country. Released his first album *Rasta* on Upright Records.

PETE ZERO: Member of the outlawed Minstrel Tendency and cannot be found in the yellow pages. Songs and stories accompanied by guitar, castanets and funny hats. Sexual politics and humour. A record and song book *Disposable Tissues* published. New title *The Performer's Fear of the Gong.*

"CONTRIBUTORY NEGLIGENCE . . . "

Hitching up the M11
coming back from an Upstarts gig
got picked up 'bout half eleven
by this bloke in a funny wig
flash Mercedes, new and gleaming
deep pile seats and deep seat piles
I got in and sat there scheming
while the fat cat flashed me smiles

Told me he was back from sessions
with a load of Whitelaw's hacks
told me he'd made no concessions
to the bootboys and the blacks
said he thought that it was stupid
fuss 'bout rapists on the news
bloke was only playing Cupid
girls like that they don't refuse

Asked me if I thought him enemy
asked me if I bore a grudge
told me that he came from Henley
said he was a High Court judge
I asked him to stop a second
'need a slash' that's what I said
when he did the anger beckoned
and I smacked him in the head

took the keys and took his money
smashed the car into a ditch
though he moaned 'they'll get you, sonny!'
got away without a hitch
I don't think they'll ever find me
'cos I'm many miles away
but if one day they're right behind me
I know what I'm gonna say –

He asked for it! He's rich and snobbish
right wing, racist, sexist too!
Fat and ugly, sick and slobbish
should be locked in London Zoo!
He wanted me to beat him up!
It was an open invitation!
Late at night he picked me up –
an act of open provocation!

High Court judges are a blight
they should stay at home in nice warm beds
and if they must drive late at night
should never pick up Harlow Reds!
A five pence fine is right and proper
and to sum up my defence
it was his fault he came a cropper
CONTRIBUTORY NEGLIGENCE!

Attila the Stockbroker

Drama, Drama, Drama, in The Launderaunderama!!!
Man came in,
putta baby in the spin-dryer
heard the little bleeder yell
till he shut the lid
Woman there said
Here! You can't put that in there!
It's not fer yumans
It's fer clothes
It won't work wiv one of those
Hadda doubt
took it out
put it in his pocket
then he shamefaced out
Laundry ladies sat and stared
censor eyes and bouffant hair
I told him yes I said,
you was there
and so was Ethel,
can't dry them
much too brittle
machine stops and starts to whistle
No can't dry them
can't dry those
must be foreign I suppose
Everybody knows
if you puttem inna spin-dryer
steada by a gas fire
babies get morose.

P.R. Murry

DRAMA,
DRAMA,
DRAMA IN THE
LAUNDERAUNDERAMA!!!

EAGLE

I am an eagle
I live in a zoo
I don't like it much
Neither would you

I sat on my perch
I glared down at crowds
Dived in my mind
Between dreamed clouds

I sat on my perch
I stared at the wall
But I saw a sky
With no bars at all

I sat on my perch
I shat on the floor
I tried to imagine
What it feels like to soar

Then God of Eagles
Made good luck for me
One unlocked moment
Enough to fly free

Life without a cage
Was too short and sweet
Wide London skies
Killed dogs to eat

I sat in my tree
Didn't know what to feel
I kept dreaming of bars
And regular meals

I sat in my tree
Alone with the sky
I saw a warm cage
I'd no wish to fly

I sat in my tree
I knew I was tamed
No move to escape
When the dart gun was raised

I am an eagle
I live in a zoo
Don't like it much
Neither would you

P.R. Murry

FRAME *UP*

It was late afternoon
When two wicked men
Rise up, Rise up against I
Dem a try fi belittle
I man integerity
Dem a try fi definate
I man charactar

One wicked man say
Im find tefin goods
Inna I office
Im run go tell
Hedda security
Dem call I
Inna dem office
One wicked man seh

Wi make a search
And find stolen goods
Inna yu office

I seh, I man is Rastafari
I god will not
Give I more than I can bear

If I is guilty
I man will pay
But first, Show I the proof
Of I guilt

Wi run go a office
Wi look
Wi no si, stolen goods
Wi look high
Wi look low

Still no si stolen goods
Dem look pon each adda
Dem go red inna dem face
Now I man no
Dem wicked will do
Anything to anyone
Fi get promotion.

Markus Jahn

TAKE UP *YOUR* **ARMS**

Take up your arms . . .
And come . . .
Take up your arms . . .
And come . . .

The suffering of eaightteen . . .
Point nine genaration . . .
Of black people . . . in this
Western hemisphare . . .
Cannot . . . an . . . will not . . .
Be wipe away . . . so easily . . .

So take up your arms . . .
And come . . .
Take up your arms . . .
And come . . .

Too many children . . . are die . . . ing
Too many mothers . . . are crying
Too many fires . . . are burning
Too many political . . . fools
Use . . . ing my people . . . black people
To feed thair egos . . .

So take up your arms . . .
And come . . .
The SWP . . . gatto stop them . . .
Take up your arms . . .
And come . . .
Anti . . . Natzi League . . . gatto stop them . . .

Markus Jahn

SUPERSTAR ON GUITAR

Hail Prince Leroy how are you
I don't see you for a year or two,
cool said Leroy cool I say
then Prince Leroy went away,
Hail Prince Leroy come back here
we use to run wild out there
in the blues dance in the ghetto
don't tell me that you forget now.

Leroy move forward to I
Leroy have on short and tie,
Leroy looking very slick
he now walk with walking stick,
Leroy said say who you are
I can say I am superstar
I found fame with my guitar
go and ask my manager.

I said Leroy this don't matter
we can still be cool together
we can still sing songs of praise
Leroy looked slightly amazed,
I said Leroy think again
don't let money buy your brain
don't let stardom buy you out
Leroy man don't mek me shout.

Leroy stood next to a wall
this is how the mighty fall,
Leroy said I now live good
I have a house of brick and a cottage of wood,
I have a real fast car and a real slick chick
I can earn my money quick,
I take 'coke' and go to mars
I have gold like chocolate bars.

Check this all you Leroys now
he who rise must fall somehow,
nice of you to play guitar
but why should you turn superstar?
hope your guilt now burns inside
have you lost your ghetto pride?
Leroy now is superstar
one time Leroy was my spa.

Benjamin Zephaniah

THAT ADJA GOIN DINIT

That adja goin dinit?
Good idea of god woden it?
Give isself the option
put up all these stars an planets
infinite fuckin millions
then when one of em snuffs it
ees got plenty more
get my meanin?

LOUD NOISE

That adja goin dinit?
fought the end of the world ad come!
You dream and dream and trancelike
dream of great catastrophies
extinction
switching off the light, pump, feeling
no moment to know there is no more
that anaesthetic darkness is complete and all
no last word
tick tock
ti

LOUD NOISE

That adja goin dinit?
fought the end of the world ad come!
Nah ee woden do that woodee
not after alls bin written about him
not after sendin is own son
not after all those people
tryin ter be like him!
Well I mean what a waste of time that wooder bin!
fer him, and fer all of them
and come to that
fer us an all
and our kids
and their kids after them an all

LOUD NOISE

That adja goin dinit?
fought itd appened that time!
Stopped yer smiling!

And what about
ART?
That adja dinit werent expectin that was yer
I mean all those pictures showin god an jesus
heaven an angels
Id feel right conned if I died
and there wasnt none
OK
I was raised on famous art

where I felt lifted up to where
beautiful women and handsome men
showed me what love and heroism and duty was.
I was raised on hollywood movies
when the bad guys regretted theyd done bad things
or theyd get what was coming to them
and the good guys were strong and honest
and the girls were beautiful dolls that cried
and for whom they shot it out
and kissed in the end
and news that said what bastards commies were
near bad as nazis that we had fought the war about
enemies of freedom.

LOUD NOISE

      That adja goin dinit?
      no? well the next one will
      seen one seen em all.
Anyway this is the point Im making
dont go out givus a minute
this chernenko and reagan
and the rest
I trust them.
No I mean it
I mean you have to dont you?
you cant do anything about them
One day one of those silly buggers
is going to fire a hydrogen bomb
if not because of some palestinian
sino soviet south american gulf
or cuban cock up
because of a computer error
then we all go up.

LOUD NOISE

      Bring down the shutters
      and the blinds
      Stop that baby coming
      with its head just out the womb
      Port hole PLINK
      Arse hole FUNT
      Eye hole bunged with a cork
All those souls blasted to never never
because we trusted god
no wonder ee gave isself the option
of having a load more ter be goin on with
when our planet snuffs it.
I woden half laugh if they all went up
put is nose out of joint
Do you believe in

Emile Sercombe

ARE *YOU*
SATISFIED?

Does the life your living seem a little dry
Are you disappointed with your piece of pie
Do you think you should have made a better score
Are you satisfied with what you settled for

Do you get up early just to walk the dog
Have you started praying? Do you dance or jog?
Do you worry much about the 3rd World War
Are you satisfied with what you settled for

Maybe it's time to make your mind up
Maybe your time is running out
Will you be asking as you wind up
Just what the fuss was all about

When the two of you are side by side in bed
Do you ever wonder what is in her head
Do you think of knocking at another door
Are you satisfied with what you settled for

Are you sick and tired of the same old scene
Has domestic bliss become a dull routine
Have you had enough or do you want some more
Are you satisfied with what you settled for

Fran Landesman

NIGHTWATCH

It is nighttime in the oldest part of the city
Where the oldest profession
is beginning the late shift.
Down the dark narrow passageways
too small for strangers to pass without touching,
windows bathed in infra-red
Display their goods,
Ultra-violet bikini ladies
yours for just 100 guilders.
They look bored,
Watching the public watching them
With eyes too curious to stare.
Spending the time between clients
Reading, smoking, polishing their nails, combing their
   hair.
Outside the church bell chimes eleven
Business is picking up
As curtains are drawn all over the city.
The days debris floats silently away
In the green water of the old canals.
Garish flashing lights beckon the wide eyed tourists.
Live fucking show, you want straight or gay,
We have books, what you like,
We got animals, children, we got everything.
They also got junkies,
Spotty young kid huddled in a doorway
Trying to keep out the cold and the wind
With a thin torn bomber jacket
With Cockney Rejects scrawled on the back.
Swaying precariously overhead hangs a sign,
"Welcome to Amsterdam".

Bernie Cunnane

Into the launderette where bedsit young trendies
soak semen soaked sheets in suds
Into missile bases where the peoples militia
destroy the silos of death with songs of peace
Into the jungle night where the tiger who has not been told
tigers rarely eat man roams in search of human flesh
Into the bedroom where bodies are rising and falling back —
the sweet sweat flesh of human surrender
Into the mushroom cloud where radiation is denied
by a unified humankind mind — one world, one peace
lasting forever

Into the dungeon where the prisoner counting days to his
freedom
meditates on space
Into the racing pit where the low slung, sleek engined cars
await their human cargo of speed
Into the sewers where rats grow fat on excrement & darkness
Into darkness itself where it's impossible to tell where
you entered, where you can leave

Into the summer of 76, thirty seconds before the Sex Pistols
take the stage at the 100 club
Into the darkened arena at Earls Court before Bob Dylan
walked out and gave the word
Into the last concert Janis Joplin ever gave imploring
with great tenderness, "don't you turn your back on love"

Into the raining night of Texas travelling across American
highways by greyhound bus
Into the mountains where climbers go forward simply
    because
it is so much better than turning back
Into the houses of parliament where the crusty fools
grow fat on gin & tonic and mackerel lunches
Into bedrooms of despair where failed marriages turn
to set the alarm
Into the poetry reading where punters shuffle in dry seats
waiting for the drum to beat
Into the head of a young poet singing with some great work
that will finally teach mankind the path to love
Into the revolution inside the revolution where men & women
stand shoulder to shoulder at the barricades and advancing
armies
are defeated by mass hypnosis

Into the universities where the only lesson on the curriculum
is contempt for our 'leaders'
Into hospitals where patients refuse to believe in illness
and walk out free into the sunlight
Into the factory where a spanner is thrown in the works of
drudgery
and someone passes round a photograph
of a river teeming with trout

Into the trout farms where trout collectivise
to resist being fished
Into the badger set where a patient kind of philosophy
is practised

Into North America when the proud Indian fished, hunted,
farmed
and lived in peace

Into the heady air of freedom walk men, women, animals
creatures that belong to the sky, reptiles that slither or wriggle
bugs that buzz

Into the ocean where giant whales and leaping dolphins
nudge the endless horizon

Into the limitless stretches of human imagination where
    cowboys
ride forever into nuclear free sunsets and the silos of death
are replaced by adventure playgrounds

Into the arms of one human being who truly loves another

Wipe the pages of history clean — this is where we begin . . .

Patrick Cunnane

U SEE

u see

you're not drifting off

u see

you're not floating away

u see

eyes like plankton phosphor in the dark
brain — jelly fish
heart — octopus
stomach — whale
genitals — tuna fish and oyster
feet — plaice and flounder
u are all over the place
constantly going up and down

u see

Christopher Cardale

FOR PEOPLE WHO DIE IN PRISONS

some birds of prey are strung so high on sight and flight
that cages round them dont touch them but slice them,
whose wings stretch wider than our horizons.
some cats flame so fierce they melt cold mountains and burn up
instantly in zoos.
even amongst broken horses some earth pounders demand
respect,
and humans for all their new instrumentation are trapped in
old conventions, still unborn.

not like the animals including horses
with different skins wedded to muscle
and muscle wedded to bone
amongst embedded nebulae —
because nerves are stars exploding
in a space of hormone.

so plain animals run together,
continue studding, neighing, thudding,
and offspringing to better offspringing
on the bouncy grave of the past,
joining races simply for the joy of running fast,
running to another, to love, to be free.

Indians understand. they include horses.
they are plain animals, who breathe the same air,
and in their big heart bravery win respect,
and the joy of running among buffalo floods —
red dust, sharp sweat, smoke in the rippling heat haze
under white light, a burning nipple in a blue breast sky.

each time they eat they kill a god,
a for giving god who whoops when the arrow sings,
and bellows a short lived loneliness on his knees,
crashing to the grass, they are the harvest of.
Indians understood, or did not, but whole tribes rotted
in a world whose iron bars enforce its difference.

Christopher Cardale

CAREERS RAP

In the first year
they put us into
various houses
and awarded points for excellence in work
and deducted points
for absences from uniform
and made it all seem
terror-bully serious,
And the wheels turned on
(The wheels turned on.)

In the second year
they took us on a tour
of LESNEYS factory
down in darkest Stratford
where they make the Matchbox motorcars
and when we left
they gave us presents
of the cars with globby paint
or bent and buckled wheels,
And the wheels turned on
(The wheels turned on.)

In the third year
we were visited by a
man from the GPO
(telecommunications)
who told us boys with an interest in science
could discover much down holes,
in the middle of the Mile End Road,
And the wheels turned on
(The wheels turned on.)

In the fourth year
we were visited by
the army and the navy
and we went to BARCLAYS BANK
where they showed us the ping pong table
as great staff relations

In the fifth year it was
CAPITAL RADIO JOBSPOT
Pharaoh and sons of
Croydon require 40,000
young people to help
erect pyramids as part
of a youth opportunities
programme.

In the sixth year
I finally got a job and now I'm
BUILDING BRITISH INDUSTRY
BUILDING BRITISH INDUSTRY
BUILDING BRITISH INDUSTRY
BUILDING BRITISH INDUSTRY
(not as interesting as it sounds this)

BUILDING BRITISH INDUSTRY
BUILDING BRITISH INDUSTRY
BUILDING BRITISH INDUSTRY
BUILDING BRITISH INDUSTRY
BUILDING BRITISH INDUSTRY
(REPEAT UNTIL VOICE OR ECONOMY BREAKS DOWN!)
Alan Gilbey

A few years ago the kids all used to get told:

"Come on sunshine, do your homework, get your 'O' levels, get a job, do well, make some money, do your parents proud." But who's got the nerve to say that to a kid now? The only advice anyone gives a kid now is get a good nuclear bunker. And in a few years time all the kids will get from their teachers and parents and the telly and papers will be:

"Sunshine, when that four minute warning siren goes off make sure that you've prepared for it, so that those four minutes are the happiest of your life." And all over the world people will be meticulously planning every second of their last four minutes, making sure it's the most glorious, ecstatic four minutes they ever lived.

Breweries will make a special beer, 250% proof, three sips and you're paralytic, who gives a fuck about your liver when there's only four minutes left. Bakeries will make a doughnut that's so full of cream and jam and fat and lard and muck and gunge that one bite and you put on half a stone in weight. Who cares about your figure in the last four minutes? Multinational corporations will be set up everywhere making products specially for the last four minutes.

Being handsome's far too boring
When you've heard that nuclear warning
You've been pretty all your life
To suit your girlfriend or your wife
Buy 'Ugliness' just spray and watch as
You come out in big green blotches
Be rancid, vile, have no respect
Don't miss the only chance you get

Swimming pools will be built, not to be opened until the warning goes off, for all the people who've always wanted to go swimming but are too ashamed of what they look like in swimming trunks. And discos will be built all over the country, not to be opened till you hear that siren, for all the people who've always wanted to dance at discos but are too scared because they can't do a proper disco dance. And people will start to fret.

"When's it going to go off then? When's it going to go off so we can do all these exciting things, and use all the wonderful things we've been spending all our money on?"

And people will start reading the overseas news column in the Guardian. Every little skirmish in the middle east, every dying dictator in South America, every little border clash in South East Asia, could this be it, could this be it? And then people will get impatient. There'll be public meetings, collection sheets, pressure groups, demonstrations.

"Today four and a half million people marched from Hyde Park to Trafalgar Square."

'What do we want?'
'Four minute warning'
'When do we want it?'
'Now'
'What do we want?'
'Nuclear war'
'When do we want it?'
'Now'

"Today it was announced that membership has passed the fifteen million mark for the Campaign for Nuclear Dismemberment."

And in the end all the international pressure will get just too much for the governments of the world.

"Well it's got just too much now hasn't it?" (push)
WAAAAAAAAAAAAAIIIIIIIIIIIIIIIIEEEEEEEEEE . . . . . .

Mark Steel

SOLDIERS

*We can't accept
that soldiers are people
until we find them dead
in our living rooms.*

*We can't accept
that soldiers are people
until we find them alive
talking to their photographs
on lonely nights.*

*We can't accept
that warriors are slaves
impotent and omnipotent
as close to God
as we'll ever be.*

Kevin Coyne

I woke from a windless dream
with burning legs
carrying pictures of war
in my toes

I laughed on the settee
at the impossible imaginings
of all my contemporaries

I woke from a windless dream

The beer was good that night.

BEER

Kevin Coyne

AFRICA I SEE

Africa, oh Africa, I see. Africa, oh Africa, be free. (chorus)
I listen to Africa and what do I hear
Machine guns cannon tanks and jets
I look over Africa and what do I see
Young mothers mourning the loss of their kids
I walk across Africa and what do I find
The millions of bodies the armies left behind

(chorus)

I listen to Africa and what do I hear
The voices of liars men without care
I look over Africa and what do I see
Misleaders and puppets preventing our liberty
I walk across Africa and what do I find
That the land of my fathers is not really mine

(chorus)

Children of Africa open your eyes
See who is laughing laughing as you cry
Children of Africa open your eyes
See who is smiling living as you die

(chorus)

Africa oh my mother why are you so blind
To see you are the victim in a monsterous crime
From East and from West you're buying doctrines of hate
And your children inherit a legacy of death

(chorus)

Spartacus R.

26

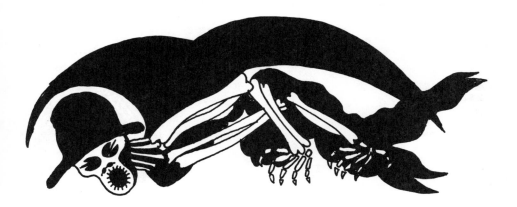

Homo erectus approached me on a railway platform.
Strange evil creatures were carved into the skin on his arms.

He had only perfected the art of walking, was low on
characteristic charms.

Long limbs protruded, painfully it seemed from his
ill-fitting garments.

Just a nose divided touch, then he spoke.
I could not conceal surprise it widened my eyes.
But I knew, that this was no joke.

He said in his own way that he took umbrage to my existence.
Wanted to punch various parts of my anatomy,
wipe the earth with my face.

From an early age, I had perfected the art of running.

Owen O'Neill

LIFE *ON* **EARTH**

I   AM   A   BLOCK   OF   FLATS
Made of a thousand and ten doors
a thousand and ten spy-holes
a thousand and ten airy spacious

                 double-locked rooms.

I'm not like that block of flats

                 down the road.
                     I'm hard.

Live in me and people'll
Be afraid of you.
Live in me and you'll be

                     afraid.

You can put my children
In approved school.
But just try it with me.

Your case won't stand up in court
They're shit-scared too.

Scared of temples and towers
And sheer glass turds of concrete.

You can scar me and mark me
And mess up my gear
But you can't
Destroy me

             you little cranedriver.

Don't mess with the cheap and effective
Don't mess with the killer.

Mike Belbin

Jagged Iron
Jackboots on my gagged soil
crimson-carpeted indeed
Soaring heat
Pregnant clouds
Over Soweto set ablaze
Whips drunken with blood
hissing sounds
jerking guns
bodies rolling
the ultimate kiss of life

Soweto
galloping nostrils
pounding hearts
Millions of paving stones
beating the milky wings of Death
Crystal clear songs rising
songs kneaded with
tears and blood and mud
but as beautiful
as a bouquet of suns
dipped in morning dew

Soweto
We counted our dead
and carefully picked a few fingernails
broken limbs
split skulls
a pair of eyes
and every piece of torn flesh
we could find
and buried all

Then we sat and wept and sighed then sang
As we rose
it was suggested
we went back to build barricades
around each drop of blood
our fallen heroes left behind
lest some impure feet
tread upon our sacred memory

Soweto
Flesh ripped by the shot
heads hitting gun-butts
ribs bare as poverty
into bayonets
Tear-gas smoky-graved indeed
Wrestling with the
whirling dust in Soweto
Today, Today is a feasting day
for the wild beast
And again the icy claws of
Death have sunk many a black heart

but again, but again our songs have risen
as pure as the morn
bold as Steve Bantu Biko
strong as the people who sing them
deep as the yawning gutter
where one day
the foe will lie silently still
the gutter
his natural habitat

Ahmed Sheikh / African Dawn

EL SALVADOR

Tierra de Sangre
Tierra de muerte
Tierra de vida
En el Salvador
Mas que nunca la Revolution
En la memoria de todos
que luchan cada dia
Para la liberacion national
Contra El Imperialismo Americano
del Yankee animal
La Revolucion en el Salvador
Tierra de Sangre
Tierra de muerte
Tierra de vida

El Salvador
Rattling Guns
Breaking Rocks
Exploding Bombs
Shattering Glass
Dangling Chains

El Salvador
Deafening cries of pain
Echoes of a motherless midnight cry
Convulsions of a dying child
Cracked marble pedestals of love
Jackboots on your padlocked lips
Whistling shells
Groaning souls

El Salvador
The sun above you bleeds
Thundering clouds are pelting down hail stones
And there is nowhere to hide
El Salvador
Your landscape is simmering Red
Waiting to catch the fire that glows in your heart
El Salvador
Death creeps thru the narrow alleyways of your
    shanty towns
And blood runs where water ran before
And blood runs where water ran before

El Salvador
Skyscrapers touching your skies
Tin sheets knocked into wood
fixed into earth
The dove stares at horizon
But only from a cage

El Salvador
Tell me El Salvador
Are you the mountain which breaks under
    humiliation

El Salvador
Why do you search for food clutching the wind
Whilst your orchards have not been visited

You walk the dark
But I can hear you whisper songs of resistance
El Salvador
This vibrates all over the land
Clutched fists hit the citadels of power
And juntas spend their mandate
On toys which the boys love
But which kill and destroy

El Salvador
We promised you a rainbow
But when it cuts across your skies
Would you be strong enough to sing us a song
El Salvador
Please let it roar with the sound of your rivers
And echoes of your mountain caves

El Salvador
Don't forget to set it in Inca silver and smooth
    Brazilian oil
Let it be a strong baritone Chorus, El Salvador,
Soaked in melodious symphony
But not a slumbering symphony, El Salvador
Let it be one disturbed and agitated
Here and there
There and here
by memories of victorious cries
and chants of your fighters
El Salvador

El Salvador
Don't cry for me
Like Argentina or Congo
Please sing
The winds wait to carry it across the continent
El Salvador
Senegalese griots wait with freshly tuned koras
Mbira ensembles have already gathered in
    Harare in Zimbabwe
Dagomba brekete beaters wait to peel their
    skins away
When it breezes thru our neighbourhood
We promise you a thousand rainbows on a
    thousand flutes

El Salvador
The road is long and winding
But dare to struggle
And dare to win
For victory is certain
El Salvador, El Salvador, El Salvador . . .

Kwesi Owusu / African Dawn

THE **BEACH**

Grey sea, sweat without warmth.

Lumped pebbles in a mindless crest,
Slipping and shifting a few near to the water.

Low tide rank sweet salt harbour smell.

The horizon is a fleet of rusty ships
Cheering their way to the Abattoir.

Bunkers of rotting seaweed hair,
Blank unseeing eyes that peer and stare.
Detritus, dead wood and dead language.
Blobs of fish-egg, sucked little white brains
And the zero white sun behind a chemical cloud
Hangs above the Power Station, a looming
Magnified, mountain-sized

Skeletal shroud.

the price
of distance
is death.

Jay Ramsay

THERE'S NOTHING *LIKE* A **BATH** *AFTER* A **MILITARY** *COUP*

if events of the nearby past in Poland, the Middle East,
Central America, Afghanistan or (dare it be said) Greenham
Common
have caused you more concern than the recent legislative work
of Norman Tebbit and Tom King
go report to the White House or the Kremlin
cos who knows there might be
a small amount of dollars or roubles waiting for you.
not exactly a different system from the one whereby
Neil Kinnock gets absentmindedly cast
as a poor culture's makeshift messiah.

the poem goes

There's nothing like a bath after a military coup.
Have a good bath and decide what you're going to do.

Ferenc Aszmann

SMO*KING* SU*PER***MAN**

I thought you must be joking
When I heard Superman had started smoking
He's been signed up by Rothmans for their latest campaign.
To start school kids smoking again.
Back to the bike sheds with a porno mag.
They said it all started a week ago.
But the reason nobody knows.
Superman was caught in a pub with Nichoteen
Smoking merrily and acting obscene.
No more enemies but the best of mates
coughing and choking, feeling great.
No fear however, anti-smokers unite,
Show kiddies their error, show them whats right.
Margaret Thatcher doesn't smoke, or does she.
She was heard, turning to Dennis say pass the cutchie
Supermans a rebel now if you see my point
Because now he's been seen smoking a joint.

Little Dave

"POEM FOR A NUCLEAR ROMANCE"

What will it matter then
When the sky's not blue
But blazing red
The fact that I simply love you

When all our dreams lay deformed
And dead
We'll be two radio active dancers
Spinning in different directions
And my love for you will be reduced to powder

The screams will perform louder
And louder
Your marble flesh will soon be raw and burning
And kissing will reduce my lips to a pulp

Hideous creatures will return
From the underground
And the fact that I love you
Will die

You don't have to sleep to see nightmares
Just hold me close
Then closer still
And you'll feel the probabilities pulling us apart
Pulling us apart.

Anne Clark

CRIMINALS *OF* HUNGER

So we see who our enemy is —
The handshake that turns into a fist
Rich hands that never stretched to save
Hands that took but never gave . . .

The government teach us poor to be thrifty —
Us who have nothing to save —
Demand that the hungry eat less
And slave from the cradle to the grave . . .

The government help the rich
So our anger burned their private club to the ground.
We're neglected on our poor side of town.
The factories we worked in have been shut down.

Instead of promising us jobs
They gave the police more power
To enforce their laws on us suffering poor
To make us bend even lower.

Now there's war, there's hate
And they've made it illegal to demonstrate.
But we're getting together, we're not going to break.

They try to make our love afraid
Twist our arms behind our back
But we're getting together — to fight them back
We're getting together — white and black.

There are battles of the hearts and tongues (*twice*)
But they're making us fight with bricks and guns.

Nothing but that we're learning
Nothing but blood is boiling
Nothing but ourselves be raising
We're toiling, with our lives we're toiling . . .

We have lost our laughs and can't let ourselves cry (Choru
We're afraid to kill but more afraid to die
We're afraid of violence — what will violence win?
But we're more afraid to keep on living like we've been.

They don't know the ways of how we live
We are letting them feel the pains they give us.
Thou shalt not steal — their judges say it's wrong —
But that doesn't mean we won't be stolen from.

The homeless must be housed, the jobless be fed
The law protects the rich —
We must break their laws like bread.
Break their laws like bread, their laws like bread (*twice*)

We must break their laws like bread.

No longer can we bleed in quiet
Angry hearts can't peacefully riot
I can't despair — I can't swallow my grief
Like a beaten man unable to spit out his teeth.

As I stood I felt an itching all over my skin
So I smashed the plate glass window in
To take all the things my folks had been needing
And I didn't notice that my hands were bleeding.

These dark cold streets aren't paved with gold
As in children's stories we're always told
But the broken window glass it glittered
With diamonds amongst the trash and litter

Suddenly the night was a thousand telephones ringing
Electrified, sirens screaming in the air
A thousand watches were ticking, my heart beat hard
Footsteps were hard upon the stair.

With a BOOM, CRASH, BOOM
The police burst into my room
And shot at anything that moved, however small.
They shot at the tap dripping in the hall.
At the flies rioting on the wall
And at the creaking of the rocking chair
But they didn't shoot me, 'cos I wasn't there
I was gone . . .

I came as close to being black as I'll ever become
Hunted like a slave on the run
I escaped, they lost me, they'll never win me
I went like fire burning up through the chimney . . .

I'm like a disconnected telephone wire
An empty house burning on fire
Panicking for the child on the top floor
Flames are licking through under my door
Paralysing me, burning my foundations
I'm both the water from the firemen's hoses
And I'm the fire they fight burning and a-raging
Burning and a-raging.

I'm a rebel on the run
From Johannesburg to Brixton
Belfast to Kingston
Before the fascists and the pigs come.

We fought the dictator
The stoolpigeon and the traitor
The fascist hidden in a uniform
He was stopping the future from being born.

They feed us through the TV station
They feed a whole nation through the radio
The juntas got to go, change their press
'Cos they always tell less or more than the truth.

Give us black and white lies
It's the voice of the general in disguise
The general is scared and wants to see me die
So I run . . . So I run . . .

I don't want to be anyone's target
Someone ever moving that they can't hit
And someone they can't trip as I run
That they can't trap, with a will they can't crack
Faster than the bullets from their soldiers' guns. (Chorus)

But do you soldiers know your enemy
When you look through your rifle sights
At those who want bread not bullets?
We don't want you to make us fight.

Soldiers strangle or embrace the dead
If to history you are drawn
But don't strangle your sisters and brothers
Who are struggling to be born.

Like a weathercock the rebel turns and stands
Blown by winds of change from distant lands
More than just a little news he heard
More than just a message from a little bird.

From South Africa to Ireland
To El Salvador
We share the same fate, we wear the same chains
We fight the same war.

We want rights, not charity
And we need solidarity
Got to fight against our poverty
We need solidarity
To protect our community . . .

Black, white, yellow, tan
Young, old, woman and man
They'll have us fighting each other for jobs
Have us fighting like devils for the love of their god.

Rory McLeod

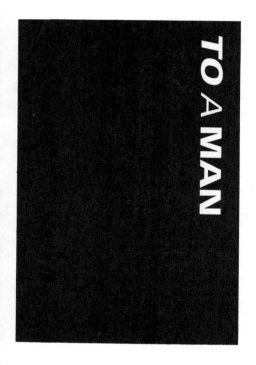

TO A MAN

you say
colour is clear
fields lie, little
tucked-up
beds of taut green silk
an orange car comes by
glossy as caramel, colts
kick up their smart white socks

I tell you
look again
brown is brighter than shorn curls
and bronze ditches
are deep with the purple of figs

the hedges' olive mouths
are stained with plums
those forests flush, that
beech-flame interrupts
the willows' silver-grey

only your language knows
where rust ends
salmon, pink begin

I tell you
landscape is truer than you
less curt
and more careless

Michèle Roberts

SOME MALE POETS

They write poems about
the softness of our skin
the curve and softness
in our eye
the declivity of our waist
as we recline

we are their peace, their consolation

they do not write of the rage
quivering

we snuggle perfection in
the ball of our foot
our hair weaves
glowing by lamplight
as we wait for the step
on the step

they have not written of
the power in

we approach divinity in
our life-source
we are earth-mother
yearned for
absent muse
shed a silent tear for
missed and loved

we are their comfort, their inspiration

sometimes we are regretted
when we behave
like a jealous woman
and loved for
our jealousy which
shows our devotion

they have not written of

and when we have begun to
speak of it, limping
coarsely, our eyes
red with sleepless pyramids

they have written of us as
whores, devouring Liliths

and never as

Michelene Wandor

THE REVOLUTION WILL BE TELEVISED

The revolution will be filmed by hand-held video camera
and broadcast in the minorities slot on Channel 4
assisted by the Arts Council
and sponsored by Hitachi and Ford.
The revolution will be threatened with legal action by Mary
    Whitehouse
and broadcast at 3 in the morning,
'slightly altered' by order of the IBA.
The revolution will be preceded by a warning
to people of a nervous disposition.
The revolution will be cinema verite
with bugs instead of flies on the wall,
mass observation and participation techniques
and hundreds of phone lines so you can call
and nominate the socialist goal of the week.
The revolution will be filmed in black and white
to create a gritty authentic feel
with amateur actors who keep fluffing their lines
and the result in doubt till the final reel.
The revolution will feature intimate sex-scenes
but the actors will be forbidden to come.
The revolution will be the subject
of a record number of viewers complaints about the outcome.
The revolution will initially be a pilot
with the possibility of a series to follow,
a book and a record of the theme tune
chatshow appearances and a commemorative video.
The revolution will be accompanied by canned laughter
— ho ho ho Ho Chi Minh,
with the peoples will credited as executive producer
and a studio discussion shortly after.
The revolution will be shot on location
in Finland Portugal and Hartlepool
with a cast representative of all sections of the community
— one eighth black, one half women, and three eighths
complete fools.
The revolution will be launched at a press lunch.
There will be after-the-match interviews
with the manager and captain of the winning team
who will both be pleased as Punch.
The revolution will be previewed in City Limits
as a brave first attempt but bound to be defeated
because it wouldn't go far enough.
The revolution will not be repeated.

Andy P. (with apologies to Gil Scott-Heron)

EM*PIRE DAY*

I'd been picked!
I'd been picked!
My arms were a flinging,
My heart was a singing
'Cos I'd been picked!
It was for Empire day
I'd been picked,
My teacher said I was
a good reader
And I could dress up
As the leader
Of the Empire
We had then.
I'd wear a bronze helmet
And be draped
In a red white and blue flag
And reign over all other lands,
That's what an Empire meant then.
The day came nearer,
I was getting excited,
Teacher spoke to me,
Then my day was blighted.
She realised I was too small
To reign.
She wanted someone tall and striking,
Who looked like a viking,
Holding a shield and looking
Across the sea.
I was already weedy,
Then I felt rather seedy,
And asked if I could go home
'Cos I was in pain.
She said I could
Do this part when I
Grew older
But how could I?
Silly old cow.
We ain't got no
Empire now!

Gladys McGee

THE NEW LAUNDRETTE

Gazing at my washing,
In the local laundrette.
Back against the driers,
Getting in a sweat.
Just one of those days,
When nothing goes right.
Your colours won't colour,
And your whites won't white.
And you gotta sign on,
At the labour exchange.
There's a queue at the spinner,
And you need some change.
And you stare at the bubbles,
Say, oh my gosh.
As you see your world,
Going round in the wash.
And the washing machines,
Go round and round.
And in your dreams,
You hear a sound —

"How do you do — what's new?
Can I help you fold your sheets?
How do you do — who're you?
So good to meet you."

I was going crazy,
I felt so tense.
When the stupid machine,
Got stuck on rinse.
And I had a feeling,
I was gonna explode.
When the spinner jammed,
On overload.
But I got to the driers,
Got my money in the slot.
They went round —
But they didn't get hot.
You know the feeling,
I lost control.
I was being sucked in,
To a wet black hole.
And the washing machines,
Went round and round.
And in my dreams,
I heard a sound —

"How do you do — what's new?
Can I help you fold your sheets?
How do you do — who're you?
Where can I reach you?"

In a world full of people,
You got no friends.
When you've got a pound note,
But you need some tens.
All my composure,
Went down the drain.
Rapid exposure,
Of all my pain.
I started shaking,
I was on my knees.

When up comes this guy,
In dungarees.
And he said . . .
"Are you into 'Primal'?
I heard you scream."
I said "I think it's 'Persil',
For the modern machine".
"That's a bit aggressive",
He pointed out.
"A bit excessive,
Without a doubt".
Ouch!
I said "thanks for your help mate,
I'd better go".
I was feeling threatened,
A little macho.
But as I stumbled to the door,
I heard him say,
"Come and meet the boys"
On Saturday.
And the washing machines,
Went round and round.
And in my dreams, I heard a sound —
A CLUNK . . . and a CLICK.
And the roaring in my head stopped.

And then I woke up,
It had all been a dream.
I'd been hypnotised,
By the spinning machine.
I pinched myself,
And gave a shout — ouch!
As I realised, I was inside out.
And a terrible pun,
I couldn't squash.
Said "Don't worry son" —
"We'll all come out — in the wash".

In the new laundrette,
You never regret.
Hanging around too long.
You sing and sway, the washing day,
Cabarets along.

Pete Zero

CIVIL*I*SATION

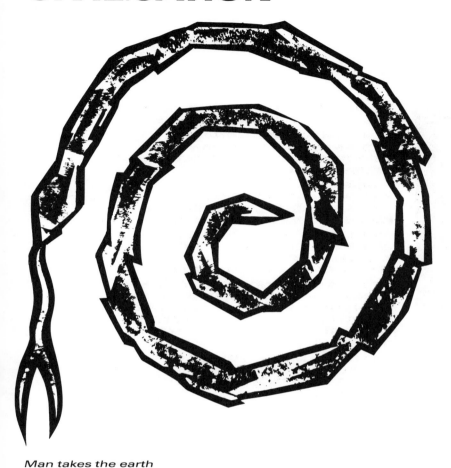

Man takes the earth
And makes it into him,
The Eiffel tower, Nelson's column, the GPO tower
Pricks are everywhere.
Woman is inferior
Let you down at the gates of Eden:
I'm sick of getting the blame
Because one fucking apple got eaten.
The UN building, the leaning tower of Pisa
But my genitalia is left to doctors and text books to mull over
What's a clitoris to you?
Compared to the Eiffel tower.

Alev

HITLER'S BIRTHDAY PARTY

PUNK, FUNK, JUNK & GETTING DRUNK.
IT'S HITLER'S BIRTHDAY PARTY.

DISCO FASCISMO, NON-STOP.
A CHANCE TO DECCA-DANCE.
A PROPER WAGNER BLITZKRIEG BOP
IN LEATHERED ELEGANCE.

FUHRER IN A PAPER HAT.
THE WITTIEST OF BLOKES.
A CHARLIE CHAPLIN LOOK-ALIKE
WHO'S TELLING JEWISH JOKES.

A KILLER DOWN THE KELLER –
SMASHING SENSE OF HUMOUR.
A LOVELY LITTLE FELLOW . . .
IF YOU IGNORE THE RUMOUR

OF TEN KOMMANDANTS' TORTURY
IN BEER-&-BORTSCH DEBAUCHERY
WITH LOTSA SMOKE & SMACK & COKE
AT HITLER'S BIRTHDAY PARTY.
THE FASCIST THING. THEIR ANNUAL FLING.
IT'S HITLER'S BIRTHDAY PARTY.

ARYANS & HITLER YOUTH,
ANGELS, SKINS & GOYS –
SOPHISTICATED & UNCOUTH,
ELITE, EXOTIC BOYS.

AND SAVAGE GIRLS IN UNIFORMS
WHO MINGLE IN THE SPREE.
A MILITARY BAND PERFORMS
& ALL THE DRINKS ARE FREE.

JOY DIVISION JEWESS JOBS
FOR ALL THE MEN IN BLACK –
JUNKERS JUNKIES, MOSLEY MOBS
& S.S. MEN IN MACS.

THEY SHOW THE FILM HE'S MADE, Y'KNOW –
'MEIN KAMPF : PART 2' – ON VIDEO.
THERE'S LOTSA SEX & TOTAL WRECKS
AT HITLER'S BIRTHDAY PARTY.
PRICKS & KICKS & COCKTAIL STICKS
AT HITLER'S BIRTHDAY PARTY.

IT'S JUST BEGUN. THERE'S BIGGER FUN
FOR HITLER'S BIRTHDAY PARTY.
THERE'S MUCH, MUCH MORE – LIKE TOTAL WAR!
AT HITLER'S BIRTHDAY PARTY.

Nick Toczek

THE **FUNERAL** *OF* *FATHER*

Black,
They all wore black.
Even the cat wore black.

Flowers.
Wreaths of flowers.
Gardens of flowers
for him who only grew vegetables.
Mother.
Mother wept
forgetting the black eyes he gave her.
And brother,
my brother didn't care
to remember the beatings.
Only I spat on the coffin
as it dropped
and said something
my sister wouldn't tell the vicar,
who, while reading the service,
scratched his nose.
And that was the end of Father.

Back home we drank
the sherry from under the stairs.
Aunt Flo remembered early years
when Father was a lad.
I smiled,
infamous by now
for my lack of gravity.
I smiled and said aloud,
"He was the biggest bastard
you ever knew,"
and then,
as the clock passed one,
they had an honest moment;
nobody denounced
the prodigal son
with his two-tone shoes.
That was the memory of Father.

Denise King

A MODERN SONG OF SONGS

Oh that you would kiss me
with the kisses of your lips!
For your love is better than hash.
I am a rose of Peckham,
a lily of the housing estates.
As a lily among brambles
so is my love among unemployed school-leavers.
My beloved is like a gazelle
or a young stag in his Alfa Romeo
bounding over the hills of Dulwich.
My beloved is all radiant and ruddy,
distinguished among young offenders,
his body is better than sniffing glue.
His speech is most sweet
and he is altogether ace.
This is my beloved
and this is my friend
O daughters of Peckham.
My beloved has gone to his gardens,
to the beds of marijuana;
to pasture his Suzuki in the allotments.
I am my beloveds
and my beloved is mine;
he pastures his old Suzuki
amongst a pensioner's radishes.
I am my beloveds
and his desire is for me.
Come my beloved
let us go forth to Peckham Rye Park
and lodge in the Flower Garden,
let us go forth late to the Flower Garden.
There you can lay with me
and pull up all the marigolds.
Make haste, my beloved,
and be like a gazelle in your Alfa Romeo
upon the hills of Dulwich.

Denise King

THE **BACK**SLAP**PERS**

What greater secrecy of love
than the cracked tiles of the
boys' room where faucets drip,
bored to tears with tales of
girls succumbing? Through the
smoke rings they gather, nodding
and jerking their heads as they
lie about the ease they had in
breaking down the barrier of
mother-tightened pant-elastic.
The most graphic, his laugh
caught short, his fag suspended,
recalls her eyes bulging as he
led her to the haven of a darkened
garage, bulbs smashed to the oily floor,
past the gleam of elbow-greased cars
reflecting her illease as he led
her to the teastained mattress
erected to the worship of debasing.
His doubts are chased away as
he fills his lungs, assured that
they both enjoyed it.
Another deals the cards on spittle
and in a reversal of sight sees
his hand calloused and yellowed with
tobacco running through her hair,
diverting knots, smells the stench
of beer covering her face, regurgitated
later behind someone's fence like the
words he tells them all.
He feels the slither of his lips
smearing her sister's lipstick,
inexperienced and unwilling to learn.
But as he deals a king he ignores
the memory of her after-fumble tears,
the way she grabbed up her clothes
and tripped as she ran.
Those sitting on sinks, in front of
various phone numbers, simply smile
and count their belt loads
of broken hymens, doubtless.

Jennifer Mitchell

I *SHALL* VOTE **SDP** *BECAUSE* . . .

I shall vote SDP because
deep down I want to live in Surrey

I shall vote SDP because
I believe Wales should be turned into an industrial
archaeological museum,
Scotland into a safari park (or a thousand hole golf course)
and Ireland should be an agricultural district of England

I shall vote SDP because
we are all centre and no circumference
but we will be alright once we find somebody to blame

I shall vote SDP because I believe
the neutron bomb is just a sort of atomic bailiff
I shall vote SDP because private health schemes
are the only way to survive the bomb

on a personal note, I shall vote SDP because
I wear y fronts (the last letter in my alphabet)
and even though I vote SDP, I am well qualified
to be an MP myself, being a strong swimmer

I shall vote SDP because
I want to write mildewed articles for the Guardian
I shall vote SDP because
I believe in bigdrum banalities

I shall vote SDP because
England should be middle class
(I know I am because my body stops at the waist)
and I shall vote SDP because
I don't believe in class *therefore* it doesn't exist

I shall vote SDP because
I believe in making self-interest patriotic
because I believe in keeping politics out of politics
but most of all I shall vote SDP because
the trouble with Socialism
is it interferes with greed

Donal Carroll

ENGLAND'S OWN

God is alive & well
& living in England
but he's fat
& gone to seed
with all the bread & wine
he'll ever need,
he wears a dog collar
& a lead
& you can tell
he knows his place
by the footprints
on his face,
if you catch him praying
he'll be saying
our Margaret
who art insane
Thatcher be thy name
thy bootboys come
& thy will be done
in the real world
as it is in Finchley
give us this day
our daily shitkicking
& forgive us our scepticism
as we forgive those
who read the *Sun*
& lead us not
into annihilation
but deliver us from Reagan
for thine is the kingdom
the power & the majority
& bollocks to Jesus
Amen

Pat Condell

THE PUB TEAM IN *MAJORCA*

fifteen of them by the hotel pool
in sawn-off levis
pink chests & conspicuous knees
& big fat Bimbo coming down to sunbathe
in a boiler suit with the legs sheared off
the only thing that will fit him

"I'm a fuckin fool to me fuckin sen, me
I could lose a stone in a week
but I eat six meat pies
just standing in t'chippy queue
no wonder I'm so fuckin fat"

& they put in twelve hour shifts at the bar
waiting for the nymphos to materialise
& the one with the biggest mouth gets sunstroke
claims he can't feel a thing
but you can see him glowing in the dark

"you're a flash cunt, you
a cocky bastard & all,
& this fuckin beer's piss
when we get home you wait
it's straight off t'fuckin plane, me
not muckin about with fuckin customs
straight through customs
straight into t'fuckin taxi
down t'fuckin pub
ten fuckin pints!"

& he spends the rest of the week
in his rum-sodden room
with the blinds drawn
throwing up
moaning

& at the club el Cid
looking for dagos to sort out
they're beaten to pulp by a Finnish ice hockey team
who just happen to be sitting there
in their blazers
sharing an orange juice
doing crosswords

"it weren't our fault
Cappy got chucked on their table
& the whole fuckin place went mad"

& one of the lads has a skin disease
it comes off him in flakes
he rubs creams & lotions on his face at night
but you hear them talking at the breakfast table
"it were like a fuckin blizzard in our room this morning"

the poor sod can't get anyone to dance
with ointments covering the map of the moon
that used to be his face
he pulls scared, rigid typists off their chairs
"come on luv, I won't do owt"

Pat Condell

CH*ILDREN*

*The children are playing a game of chase
and one of the children who seems to want to be chased after
calls out above the screams and laughter
don't chase me,
don't chase me!
and nobody does.*

John Hegley

*CHILD*REN
WITH **ADULTS**

My auntie gives me a colouring book and crayons.
I begin to colour.
After a while she looks over to see what I have done and says
you've gone over the lines
that's what you've done.
What do you think they're there for, ay?
Some kind of statement is it?
Going to be a rebel are we?
I begin to cry.
My uncle gives me a hanky and some blank paper
do your own designs he says
I begin to colour.
When I have done he looks over and tells me they are all very
good.
He is lying,
only some of them are.

John Hegley

LYING HERE

lying here, next to you
in the crook of your shoulder
breathing together
happy together
its very romantic
just like in the films
but i'm going to have to move soon

its nothing against you
so i hope you wont be offended
its just that i'm uncomfortable
i can't sleep on my back
never could
can only sleep on my side
so i'm going to have to move soon

i've never really done this before
shared a bed with someone
so i'm not too sure of the procedure
in fact i'm rather worried
you see if i lie facing you
you might smell my breath
and i would hate that
i cleaned my teeth for about ten minutes earlier
but already i can feel it wearing off
i would hate you to go off me
because my breath smelt
but i'm going to have to move soon

on the other hand
if i lie with my back to you
i might fart against your leg
and i would hate that
i can control it quite well when i'm awake
but i don't know what happens when i'm asleep
(do people fart when they're asleep
or is it a waking complaint?)
i would hate you to go off me
because i farted against your leg
but i'm going to have to move soon

i've just had an idea
if i lie facing you
with my head under the blankets
we won't have any problems
so i do and there we lie
me with my head under the blanket
you quietly farting
and i'm going to have to move soon.

Claire Dowie

PR*O*TEST

It was a sixtys dream
An now its a primal scream
Let's have peace not war
The future is ours
It dont belong to them
Protest lets servive.
Cos I dont wanna be dust
Or a nuclear crust
A scab on a barbed wire fence
I dont wanna be burnt
To a scarlet pink
A hairless bloody mess
I just wanna be me
An tottal free
An die at home in bed
Cos the future is ours
It dont belong to them
Protest lets servive.
Or you'll end up as dust
Or a nuclear crust
A scab on a barbed wire fence
Just a scab on a barbed wire fence
Protest you know it makes sence.

Ginger John the Doomsday
Commando

BABYLON A TURN DE SCREW

Babylon a turn de screw
Man a feel pressure
Som turn to stealing
Som start feeling fe
Run back a yard

Som seh pressure deh deh to
Babylon is Babylon is Babylon
Here, dere an everywhere
Turning de screw — confusing
You You and You

An wen yu her pon de shout
Madness — Madness — Madness

Babylon a turn de screw
Papa get de sack
No work — No pay
An dole money noh nuff
Mama feel de shack
We have fe stap eat meat
Noh good shoes pon we feet
An Winter a com

An wen yu here pon de shout
Madness — Madness — Madness

Babylon a turn de seten!
Three a we left school — no wock
No wock — No pay
An dole money noh nuff
Big sista a breed buoyfren naah wock
Big bredda turn to weed
Bad weed meck im feel dizzy

An wen yu here pon de shout
Madness — Madness — Madness

Babylon a turn de screw
De snatcher jus snatching snatching
Bills piling up here there an everywhere
De youths jus watching watching
Yearning Yearning Learning de hard way
Pressure reach de peak

An wen yu hear pon de shout
Madness — Madness — Madness

Frederick Williams

PEACE IN OUR TIMES

After a while
it's easy to understand
why soldiers need their wars
why it needs fighters
and peacemakers
and after that the peaceful
who can work without battles
who can see beyond the obstacles
who can walk the streets
and not look for a sniper
on every rooftop 360° of suspicion
leaves a narrowness of vision
and when life is taken in short strides
punctuated by dashes across the open spaces
all you see is another place to hide
survival is called victory
you live to fight another day
and vice versa
and in the end
when the fighting is over
you are left boxing shadows
while others toast the phoenix.

Growing up, I lived in a new town
and watched it grow with me
I listened to the developers
in the front room
and thought the world had only just begun
heads of state came from the east
and sat drinking tea
in an ordinary house
later they were assassinated
outside the town
I listened to others
and while they talked of battles and comrades
I knew they had never left the field
and I was listening to ghosts.

Later, when I returned
I found the town had passed
from the men of dreams to the shadow boxers
and as I walked
the shell of the creature dying in infancy
I wanted to shake myself free of the bedclothes
and wake up in the world I'd been promised
It's easy to understand the soldiers
and the barren landscape they inhabit
but what I want to know is
when they're finished
why don't we simply take away their guns
and lock them in cinemas watching old documentaries
while the rest of us build whatever it was
they were fighting for in the first place.

John Rowe

BURNING QUESTIONS

???

You are a lynx and a liar
and I have my father's dancing eyes
and laughter crackles between us
like snakes or lightning
in the quick dab of lip

Laughing we touch and fly
we are buzzing and crafty
Uncatchable.

Laughing we deny
what is darkest in us,
the word's strong shadow,
the need to choose

What shall we do with each other?

I know the shock of the future
and the whistling silence
I do not know you
You may be translucent
I may pass right through

Sit down and settle
Let me melt into you
You must tell me your truths
and see if I sting.

Alison Fell

TERM *B*EGINS *AGAIN*
(OSTRICH *BLUES*)

*I find myself
in bed again
with the sheets up over
my head again*

*papers collect
on my desk again
reports and memos and lists again*

*there are the
timetables in black ink
again*

*the silhouetted heads
in rows against the light
again*

*the lists again
of books I haven't read
again*

*nightmares again
of assignations missed
again*

*of students riding off
on bicycles playing bass guitars
again*

*and I oversleep
again
and again*

*I find myself
in bed
again*

*with the sheets up over
my head*

again

Stef Pixner

THE CEMENT MIXER

The cement mixer
sleeps in the hall.
Pretend it's the stereo
says the builder
and the skip is a junk
in a Chinese river
and the lorries
are the juggernaut ocean
roaring
or lions
hunting a dusty jungle,
the Dalston Junction
of the soul

Stef Pixner

It's a boy
It's a boy
   CRY
the monarchists
      monarchists
      monarchists

Should've been a girl
Should've been a girl
   CRY
the feminists
      feminists
      feminists

So little
yet so lusty
much too lusty
   CRY
the moralists
      moralists
      moralists

Good luck to the guy
Long live the little guy
   GUY FAWKES
   CRY
the anarchists
      anarchists
      anarchists

Anachronistic
Anachronistic
Royalty is not the key
to a classless society
   CRY
the communists
      communists
      communists

Rejoice at the news
Rejoice at the news
as we did in the Falklands crisis
   CRY
the cynics
      cynics
      cynics

O weep weep
for the silent voices
of the South Atlantic
   CRY
the pacifists

It's a fairy tale come true
It's a fairy tale come true
with eyes so blue
   CRY
the romantics
      romantics
      romantics

Second in line
Second in line
De unemployment line
   CRY
a Brixton youth

and dat aint cute
Jesus dat is de truth

John Agard

ROYAL POEM

61

All day within the enclosure
of Greenham Common,
the military busily
whizzed up and down
in sinister looking vehicles,
dark anonymous trucks
buzzing along the tarmac
for no clear reason,
maybe containing uneasy personnel
protecting themselves from the women —
who rise like lions after slumber
distinctly in disturbing number,
anarchic and wholly at one —
maybe in routine treks
or checks of their tophole work
to welcome the missiles,
the mightiest mock pricks
this world has ever seen,
no semen but seeds of destruction,
whose sorrowful journey
is speedy doomsday.

We held hands in a nine mile circle
round the perimeter fence,
which we had brought to life
by love and common sense
with grass-woven symbols,
messages, teddy bears, balloons,
woollen webs, roses, babygrows,
knitted bootees, poems, photos,
paper christmas trees with streamers,
many banners as the morning rising
(who is she? — Wisdom), Dutch, Norwegian,
solemn compound German from the Greens.
We planted primulas still flowering
and snowdrop bulbs in hope.
We sent round kisses and apples of peace,
hand to hand, face to face.
There was singing, dancing, picnicking —
soggy sandwiches, brandy, oxtail soup.
And the spirit was like a mountain,
old and strong.
It was a sturdy, cheerful quickening.

Dinah Livingstone

ANTI-RACIST PERSON

You're an anti-racist person,
concerned about my humble plight,
you want to help me get equality,
'cos I've had a disadvantaged life.

You believe we are multi-racial,
an dat I'm British, despite I'm black,
yet when I ask a question in de classroom,
is like yu nearly have a heart attack!

You're an anti-racist person,
you say everyone has equal start,
but when I go to you for job interview,
you look at me as if I fart.

You-like-to-watch-me-in-doc-u-<u>men</u>-tary,
set in far off place ona tv,
wearing loincloth, with native vices,
you feel concern about my crises,
but when I jump on me feet an move into your street,
yu screaming 'bout your property prices.

Yu study me in books an papers,
den yu talk to me above my head,
but while yu holding all yu fancy conf'rences,
your society is killing me dead.

You're an anti-racist person,
but excuse me if I must confess,
when I see your anti-racist policies,
I feel safer wid de real NF!

Marsha Prescod

MAY THE FORCE BE WITH YOU

If allyu want to keep yu carnival,
Wid yu jump-up, yu fete, yu roti,
An a chance to meet up wid yu key spar
Yu macumere an ting,
Who yu ain see for years,
Yu must remember —
Any gathering of black people in dis town,
Dus make dem nervous.
De only blacks who ain criminals,
Is entertainers, is sportsmen, or is police.

So.

Next year, we go bring out a band.
An we go have a maas, to end all maas.
Two hundred tousand black man, woman and chile
Dress in dark blue.
Yes, de maas we playing is 'police'
An de theme of we band is
Law an Order!

So when dey turn on de telly,
To hear about how many blacks riot for carnival,
All dey go see is
Two hundred tousand police going dung de road,
Singing, drinking rum,
Whining, dancing.
Dey ain go be able to tell,
Who is de real police,
An who is de maas police.

De press gon' go mad,
(Cos yu know how dey dus love take picture
Of police dancing up at carnival)
De Commissioner, Home Secretr'y an Prime Minister
Go declare how 'community policing'
Is a big success, and dey gon' be right,
(Because, of course, for dat day
De whole community go turn policeman!)

An, we black people,
Go get to keep we carnival.

Marsha Prescod